Drip, Drip, Drop
EARTH'S WATER

Why Is Seawater Salty?

by Ellen Lawrence

Consultant:

Shawn W. Wallace
Department of Earth and Planetary Sciences
American Museum of Natural History
New York, New York

BEARPORT
PUBLISHING

New York, New York

Credits
Cover, © Vibrant Image Studio/Shutterstock; 4, © Dmitry Naumov/Shutterstock; 5T, © NOAA/NASA; 5, © Stanislav Smoliakov/Shutterstock; 6T, © M. Unal Ozmen/Shutterstock; 6B, © Channonttennis/Shutterstock; 7, © jordeangjelovik/Shutterstock; 8, © Szabi/Shutterstock; 9, © CnOPhoto/Shutterstock; 10, © Rafa Irusta/Shutterstock; 11, © Shutterstock; 12, © NOAA PMEL Vents Program/Science Photo Library; 13, © EdStock/iStock; 14, © Ruby Tuesday Books; 15, © Blue Ice/Shutterstock; 16T, © Cosmographics; 16B, © kavram/Shutterstock; 17, © ChameleonsEye/Shutterstock; 18, © KPG Payless2/Shutterstock; 19, © bikeriderlondon/Shutterstock; 20, © tisskananat/Shutterstock; 21T, © Gayvoronskaya Yana/Shutterstock; 21, © stable/Shutterstock; 22, © M. Unal Ozmen/Shutterstock, © Ann Worthy/Shutterstock, and © Jiang Hongyan/Shutterstock; 23TL, © Lucky-photographer/Shutterstock; 23TC, © beboy/Shutterstock; 23TR, © Yuriy Kulik/Shutterstock; 23BL, © isarescheewin/Shutterstock; 23BC, © Sayan Puangkham/Shutterstock; 23BR, © Vilainecrevette/Shutterstock.

Publisher: Kenn Goin
Editor: Jessica Rudolph
Creative Director: Spencer Brinker
Design: Emma Randall
Photo Researcher: Ruby Tuesday Books Ltd

Library of Congress Cataloging-in-Publication Data

Names: Lawrence, Ellen, 1967– author.
Title: Why is seawater salty? / by Ellen Lawrence.
Description: New York, New York : Bearport Publishing, [2016] | Series: Drip, drip, drop: Earth's water | Audience: Ages 6–10. | Includes bibliographical references and index.
Identifiers: LCCN 2015040326 (print) | LCCN 2015041634 (ebook) | ISBN 9781943553228 (library binding) | ISBN 9781943553563 (ebook) | ISBN 978-1-64280-738-7 (pbk.)
Subjects: LCSH: Seawater—Composition—Juvenile literature. | Salt—Juvenile literature. | Salt industry and trade—Juvenile literature.
Classification: LCC GC121.2 .L39 2016 (print) | LCC GC121.2 (ebook) | DDC 551.46/5—dc23
LC record available at http://lccn.loc.gov/2015040326

For more information, write to Bearport Publishing, 5357 Penn Avenue South, Minneapolis MN 55419. Printed in the United States of America.

Contents

Salty Seawater

It's a sunny day at the beach, and you're swimming in the ocean.

You accidentally swallow a mouthful of salty seawater. Yuck!

The water that comes out of a faucet doesn't taste salty.

If you catch raindrops on your tongue, they don't taste like salt.

So what makes seawater so salty?

About 70 percent of Earth's surface is covered by oceans.

What Makes the Ocean Salty?

Seawater is salty because it contains tiny **particles** of salt.

In fact, there's nearly 1 teaspoon (5 ml) of salt in 1 pint (473 ml) of seawater.

The particles of salt are too tiny to see, but you can taste them.

a teaspoon of salt

If all the salt in the oceans was removed and spread evenly over all the land on Earth, how deep would it be? The layer of salt would be 500 feet (152 m) deep. That's the height of a 40-story building!

How do you think salt gets into the oceans?

Rocks and Salt

One way that salt gets into the oceans is from rocks on land.

Many types of rock contain tiny particles of salt.

When it rains, rainwater erodes, or wears away, rocks and mountains.

The rainwater carries tiny pieces of rock and particles of salt down into streams.

What do you think happens to salt particles once they are in a stream?

Rocky cliffs at the seashore also contain salt. When waves crash against cliffs, salt and pieces of rock are washed into the ocean.

Saltier and Saltier

Salt particles in a stream are eventually carried into a river.

The river may carry the salt for hundreds of miles.

Finally, the river will flow into an ocean.

All over the world, thousands of rivers carrying salt flow into Earth's oceans.

Over time, the salt in the oceans builds up.

The water in a stream or river contains salt particles but doesn't taste salty. Why? There's only a small amount of salt in it. This type of water is called fresh water.

How Salt Gets Into the Ocean

Under the Sea

Salt particles can get into the ocean in other ways.

At the bottom of the ocean is the **seabed**, which is part of Earth's rocky layer, or **crust**.

Seawater soaks into the rocky crust, where it gets very hot.

The water heats up and is then blasted back into the ocean through holes called vents.

This hot water contains salt from Earth's rocky crust.

There are also underwater volcanoes on the seabed. When an underwater volcano **erupts**, hot liquid rock and boiling water blast out from inside Earth's crust. This water contains particles of salt.

an underwater volcano erupting in the Pacific Ocean

It's not only oceans that have salty water. Some lakes do, too. Why do you think this is?

Saltwater Lakes

Why do some lakes have salt water while others have fresh water?

A freshwater lake usually has rivers flowing into and out of it.

Salt from the rivers gets carried into the lake and then out again.

However, a saltwater lake only has rivers flowing into it.

So, all the salt that gets carried into the lake stays there.

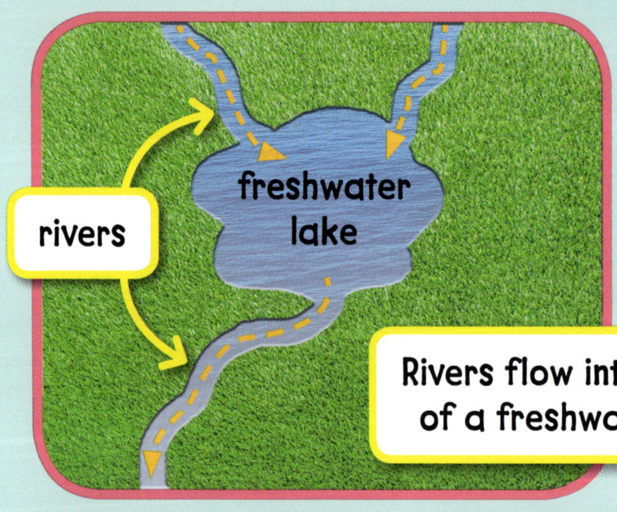

Rivers flow into and out of a freshwater lake.

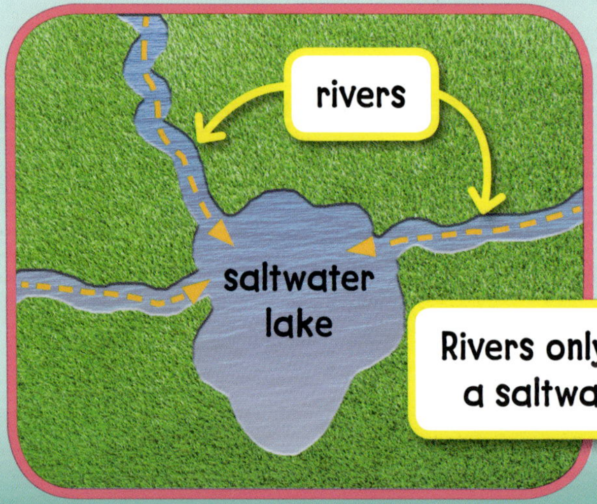

Rivers only flow into a saltwater lake.

When it's hot and sunny, some of the water in a saltwater lake **evaporates**. However, the salt particles in the water stay in the lake, which makes the remaining water even saltier.

The Dead Sea

One of the saltiest bodies of water on Earth is the Dead Sea.

The Dead Sea isn't really a sea, but a huge saltwater lake.

The water in the lake is nearly ten times saltier than ocean water!

No animals or plants can live in it because it's too salty.

That's why the lake is called the Dead Sea.

salt at the edge of the Dead Sea

People and objects can float more easily in water that has lots of salt. Visitors to the Dead Sea have fun floating in the extra-salty water.

Can We Drink Salt Water?

To stay healthy, people need to drink water.

There's a huge amount of salt water on Earth, but we can't drink it. Why?

Drinking salt water can make people sick.

The water contains so much salt that it's bad for our bodies.

Only fresh water is healthy for people to drink.

There is a way that salt water is useful to people. What do you think it is?

About 97 percent of the water on Earth is salt water. Just 3 percent is fresh water. Most of the fresh water is frozen as ice in very cold areas. Liquid fresh water is found underground and in streams, rivers, ponds, and lakes.

Earth's Water

penguins living on the ice in Antarctica

Collecting Salt

Some of the salt we put in food can be **harvested** from the ocean. How?

First, people dig shallow holes on the seashore.

Ocean waves wash into the holes, making ponds.

Over time, the water in the ponds evaporates, leaving behind salt.

Then the salt is collected and put in food to make meals tastier!

people collecting salt from a pond by the ocean

Salt that's been harvested from the sea is stored in huge mounds. Then it's packed into boxes at a factory, ready to be sold in grocery stores.

Science Lab

Some lakes become salty because lots of salt collects in the water. Let's investigate how this happens.

You will need:

- 2 teaspoons (10 ml) of salt
- A measuring cup containing 1/2 cup (118 ml) of water
- A dark-colored shallow dish
- A notebook and a pencil

How Does a Lake Become Salty?

1. Stir 2 teaspoons (10 ml) of salt into 1/2 cup (118 ml) of water in a measuring cup. Keep stirring until you can't see the salt anymore.
2. Pour the water into a dish.
3. Place the dish in a warm spot where there's lots of sun, such as on a windowsill. Keep checking the dish over the next few days and observe what happens.

What do you think will happen to the water?

What will happen to the salt?

In your notebook, write down your predictions.

How is what happens in the dish similar to what happens in a saltwater lake?

(The answers are on page 24.)

Science Words

crust (KRUST) a layer of rock surrounding Earth

erupts (i-RUPTS) shoots lava and other substances out of a volcano

evaporates (i-VAP-uh-rayts) when a liquid is heated by the sun and turns into a gas

harvested (HAR-vuh-stid) collected by people

particles (PAR-ti-kuhlz) tiny pieces of something

seabed (SEE-bed) the sandy or rocky ground beneath the ocean

Index

Read More

Lawrence, Ellen. *Polluted Oceans (Green World, Clean World)*. New York: Bearport (2014).

Leake, Diyan. *Oceans and Seas (Water, Water Everywhere!)*. Chicago: Heinemann (2015).

Owings, Lisa. *From Sea to Salt (Start to Finish)*. Minneapolis, MN: Lerner (2015).

Learn More Online

To learn more about salt water and oceans, visit
www.bearportpublishing.com/DripDripDrop

About the Author

Ellen Lawrence lives in the United Kingdom. Her favorite books to write are those about nature and animals. In fact, the first book Ellen bought for herself, when she was six years old, was the story of a gorilla named Patty Cake that was born in New York's Central Park Zoo.

Answers for Page 22

The water in the dish has evaporated. The salt has not evaporated, though, and is still in the dish. This is similar to what happens in a saltwater lake. When the weather is warm, some of the lake water evaporates, but the salt gets left behind. Then more water and salt flow into the lake from rivers, and the lake gets saltier and saltier. If you were to pour more salt water into the dish, this water would mix with the salt from your original experiment. The water in the dish would get even saltier!